Falling into Place

Praise for *Falling into Place*

A sharply observed, irreverent and poignant reckoning with human courage and vulnerability in context of lupus. Xochitl M. Perales' prose is deft, spare and brims with visuality. The afterimages extend the narrative long after one has put down the book.

> Lata Mani is a historian, cultural critic & filmmaker. Xochitl M. Perales is featured in her film, *The Poetics of Fragility*.

Xochitl M. Perales's *Falling into Place* is an important addition to the field of narrative health—an increasingly important part of the curriculum in medical schools across the nation … Rather than succumbing to all-encompassing forms of medicalization and their discontents and to the relentless and unpredictable course of this ailment, the author of this important memoir forges her own identity and presses onward ... If this memoir provides an example of the healing power of narrative in chronic individual situations that defy western restitution stories it also extends this healing to others who can partake in the journey at hand or imagine new ones that must be spoken within other lived contexts and urgencies.

Angie Chabram is professor emerita at the University of California, Davis

Even as we assume that Xochitl Perales' memoir is inviting us on an arduous journey through undeserved pain and suffering, we discover the transformative power of her writing. Riveting, evocative, inspiring, her prose lifts up the very best in all of us. A phenomenal gift to us all!

Angela Y. Davis, Distinguished Professor Emerita, History of Consciousness and Feminist Studies, University of California, Santa Cruz

Falling into Place

A Short Memoir

Xochitl M. Perales

Falling into Place:
A Short Memoir
By Xochitl M. Perales

ISBN: 979-8488208193

Cover photo by Engin Akyurt: https://bit.
ly/2T2rfPw

Contents

Prologue

During the third trimester of my pregnancy, I was diagnosed with lupus, an autoimmune illness that affects the organs and joints. The diagnosis did not come as a surprise. For weeks I had experienced unbearable pain. It hurt for me to sit on the toilet and my feet were very swollen. When I spoke to an aunt who suffered from arthritis, she told me that her aches were related to lupus flares. For years I had wondered if something was wrong with me because I would often get tired and overwhelmed with fatigue. I felt validated after receiving the lupus diagnosis from the rheumatologist.

After my son was born, the doctor prescribed 60 mg of prednisone to alleviate the lupus flare. The prednisone kept me from sleeping and caused my mind to race day and night. It was difficult for me to care for my son. I was unable to breastfeed him not only due to the prednisone but also because the hormones released during lactation made my lupus more active.

I have always been a dreamer and striven to be the best I can be. Over the years, I have discovered that surviving lupus requires honesty, grit, and a die-hard determination. I have learned to face my reality and accept my limitations. My dark sense of humor has helped me deal with the horror of my circumstances. The short memoir that follows captures three early moments of my multi-decade journey with lupus. Welcome to my life!

Xochitl M. Perales

The Death Rooms

The first day of September 2002
UCSF Medical Center
San Francisco, California

Sunday

The elevator doors open to a cacophony of sound and movement. Endless color stretches before me, a congruent backdrop to the hustle and chaos of purposefully moving bodies, blaring loudspeakers, ringing phones and rolling carts. One of the carts is being pushed by an elderly woman with bifocals, carrying large quantities of pain relief and life prolongation in liquid and pill form.

The big orderly in the pale green uniform pushes me in the wheelchair down the hall towards a long counter filled with paperwork, office supplies and phones. A couple of receptionists are swamped with various duties: sorting through paperwork, opening file cabinets, answering calls. The ritual of sameness is reflected in other hospital staff members duties, although I can't really tell who's who.

A young woman (a nurse? another orderly?) walks up to my orderly and verifies that I am "me." Before the orderly goes to his next assignment, I remember to thank him. He smiles, wishes me well and leaves. The young woman turns my wheelchair around in a different direction and wheels me a little farther before presenting me with my room.

The bed closest to the door is occupied by a young woman, perhaps in her mid-twenties. She looks Korean, or maybe Japanese. Long black hair, black eyes, smooth tan skin. She smiles and watches me with a curious expression. I smile back as I roll past her to my bed, near the windows.

The young hospital worker puts on the brakes of the wheelchair before signaling me to get up. I do so, very slowly. Next, she hands me a cotton gown from the supply closet, then closes a curtain to allow me some privacy. As I undress and put on my hospital garb in awkward motions, she introduces me to my roommate, Soo Jin, and tells us both we are here for similar reasons. The same illness, only different manifestations. Soo Jin and I are both amazed by this, and murmur appropriately.

The hospital worker leaves the room, and Soo Jin asks, "How old are you?"

"I'm twenty-nine."

"Wow. You're young, just like me. I'm only twenty-seven." She watches me with hawk eyes while I ease myself back on the bed. "Do you have kidney issues, too?"

"No." I answer, confused by the question. It's then that I notice the dialysis machine attached to her body. I quickly look away. "I get really bad arthritis, but lately I've had nerve damage, as well."

"What do you mean by nerve damage?" asks Soo Jin. "Where?"

"Well, it started with my big toe going numb a couple of years ago. Then it gradually got worse. Right now, I'm losing feeling in my left foot and both hands. That's why I'm here."

"Oh. I'm sorry," she says softly.

"I'm sure being on dialysis isn't so great either."

"No, it's not." She sighs. "Having lupus sucks."

I glance over at the monstrosity of her dialysis machine, count my blessings,

4

and say inwardly, *Amen, sister!*

A nurse is preparing to insert an intravenous tube (I.V.) below the inner crook of my right arm. I stare in horror at the jumbo-sized needle about to be plunged through layers of skin into vein. I made a decision. "I don't want an I.V.," I emphatically state.

"Sorry, but the doctor gave the order," she explains. "Besides, you need the I.V., in case there is an emergency, and we need to inject morphine into you for pain relief. That way, we don't have to go through the trouble of inserting an I.V. when you need pain relief fast."

"But I don't want morphine. I already tried it the first time I was hospitalized more than three-and-a-half years ago, and vowed never to do it again, because it made me super paranoid, and did almost nothing for the pain."

"I'm really sorry, but unless the doctor says otherwise, this goes in and stays in." Then she stabs the long, thick needle into my arm.

I absorb this intrusion of gleaming metal into my body. It feels like a violation.

I am wheeled off for various nerve tests in the late afternoon of what is still my first day in the hospital. I have my CD Walkman with me, because my stepfather, Herman, suggested that I bring along music, more than likely to keep my spirits up. I am listening to Richard Bona's *Reverence* album. I don't understand the words to most of the songs, as they are sung in the Douala language of Cameroon. But that's beside the point.

It all begins with "Invocation," a song without instruments, but with soft, earnest words dropping like raindrops on an otherwise quiet day, a chant for the spirit realm. Then comes "*Bisso Baba* (Always Together)" with its sprightly carnival feel and carefree movements. Somehow, beneath the numbness, something is stirring to life.

I am left waiting in a hallway for a little while. Tears form in the corners of my eyes. It is at this moment that my regular neurologist Dr. Scarlata, from the University of California Medical Center across the street, happens to see me.

"What's wrong?" she asks. "What are you doing here?"

I cry a little as I tell her. "I am having another lupus flare-up. This time, I have a foot-drop in my left foot, and I'm starting to lose feeling in some of my fingers on both hands – especially my left, and I am left-handed."

"Oh, honey. Don't cry. It'll be all right," she says while touching my back with her hand. I can see the warm compassion in her light brown eyes. "What are you about to do right now?"

"They're running nerve tests on me."

"Hang on. Let me find out what's going on. I'll be right back."

Meanwhile, tears slide down my face. I am amazed that they roll in a steady stream, without my having to either make noise or contort the muscles of my face. I think I've always been able to do this since I was a little girl, but I'm just now noticing it.

Dr. Scarlata returns and insists on conducting the tests herself. She took an interest in my case from the start of my illness, when I was initially referred to her about a year ago. I think part of the reason is that we are both mothers of young children and share that bond. My son, Jasim is a few months shy of four, and her daughter, a couple of months younger than him. This seemed to touch something in her when we first met. But there is also the fact that my case is more complicated case than most. I had been diagnosed with peripheral neuropathy, a condition resulting from the autoimmune disorder called systemic lupus erythematosus. Peripheral neuropathy is nerve damage in the hands and feet. Systemic lupus erythematosus, the type that I have, affects among other things, the internal organs, joints and skin.

We go into a room with odd-looking equipment. There are wires, buttons and knobs hooked up to machines. I don't pay attention as Dr. Scarlata and an assistant attach wires and taps to my hands and feet at alternating intervals. I focus instead on the sweet and lifting music coming out of my earphones. Now it is "*Muntula Moto (The Benediction of a Long Life)*" playing. The melody of the piano has a strong, heavy sound; the drums cast a steady background pulse; the guitar mimics the thick-like-syrup accent of the vocals. The song is happy. It makes me smile.

I raise my bed in order to sit up, and dial my mother's number. The phone rings four times before she picks up. "Hello," she says.

"Hi, Mom. It's Xochi."

"Oh, hang on a second." Her voice is muffled as she probably turns her head away from the phone, calling out, "Jasim! Your mommy is on the phone."

In the background, I can hear my son's sweet, raspy voice say, "My mommy's on the phone?"

"Yes. Let me talk to her for a minute, and then I'll hand you the phone."

"Okay," he says.

My mom's voice is no longer muffled when we reconnect. "Hey, Xochi. How are you feeling?"

"I'm okay, I guess. I still can't lift my foot up and my hands are getting worse. And they keep sticking needles in me – you know how much I hate needles. I really wish that they'd remove this I.V. from my arm. Other than that…" My voice trails off in mild sarcasm.

"Well, hang in there. I'm sorry you have to go through this."

"Yeah. Me, too." I can't say anything else, because hearing her concern makes my voice clog up with tears. I wait for my mom to fill the void.

"I'll let you talk to Jasim now. He's been waiting for your call."

"Yes, let me speak to him. Bye, Mom."

"Bye, Xochi. I hope you feel better."

Mere seconds go by before there is a hesitant, "Mommy? Is that you?"

"Yes, Jasim. It's Mommy."

"Are you calling from the hospital?"

"Yes, I am."

"Are the doctors giving you medicine so you can feel better?"

"They sure are."

"And are you feeling better?"

"Yes, I'm starting to feel better." It's not really the truth, but I don't want to add to his worries.

"That's good. So, when are you coming home?"

"I don't know yet, but hopefully soon. I can't stay away from my gorgeous

12

guy for too long." I can hear him chuckle a little. I say, "I miss you, sweetie."

"I miss you, too."

"I'm giving you a great big hug and kiss through the phone. Muah!" Trapping the phone between my left ear and shoulder, I reach my arms around myself and squeeze tight, as if Jasim is actually there. "I love you very much."

"I love you, too."

"I'll call you again tomorrow. Goodbye, sweetie."

"Goodbye, Mommy."

I wait for my son to hang up first. When I hear the dial tone and hang up the receiver I allow myself the luxury of crying.

My roommate, Soo Jin, is a riot. She is upbeat, despite the lupus and the dialysis, talks animatedly and makes everybody smile. On my first night there, she asks, "Did you see that fine-ass man who just checked into room 704 about an hour ago? What a hottie! I wonder if he's into lupus chicks on dialysis." At that, a couple of hospital workers and I burst out laughing.

One of them, a male nurse who works nights, later confides to me (while Soo Jin is asleep) that she checks into this hospital quite often, for any number of reasons, because she is addicted to morphine. She'll do whatever she can to get admitted here and at various other hospitals, just so she can lie in bed all day and smile in a morphine-induced stupor. All I have to do is look at the catheter permanently attached to her belly button so that she can be hooked up to her dialysis machine, and the morphine addiction makes perfect sense. It is her escape.

14

The night nurse has made several visits to my room tonight. He is a white man in his late thirties, with sandy blond hair, light blue eyes, peach skin, average height and a stocky build. He comes over on all of his breaks, or perhaps he is inventing medical reasons to see me. He brings me chocolates and conversation, offering to give me massages, which I politely decline. He assures me that getting massages is standard procedure for all the patients here, except for the really old women. I laugh a little at his comment but still say no.

In my "ordinary" life, I could easily be revolted, but in here, I am amused.

I listen to the night nurse as he shares hospital gossip with me. He is mildly entertaining with his incessant chatter and colorful stories. He tells me about the two rooms adjacent to mine, "Those rooms are used especially for our terminally ill patients." I'm not sure if he is supposed to share this information with patients, but in the blink of an eye I become obsessed with those rooms. I proclaim them the "Death Rooms."

I imagine taking a lap around the corridors to force my blood to keep circulating, as one of the other nurses suggested (even though it would be so much simpler to just lie in bed, and not get up EVER). I walk by the Death Rooms and turn my head quickly to stare through the open doors at the room's next victims. The worst part is thinking about them being empty the next day.

16

Monday

"A more aggressive approach is needed in order to halt this current lupus flare," a doctor tells me in the morning. "The best option available to you is to undergo Cytoxan chemotherapy."

I am thinking about all of those made-for-TV movies where the cancer patient is shown stumbling to the toilet, retching from the last meager meal they were barely able to swallow. "I don't like that option," I say. "The thought of putting something so toxic into my body … losing my hair … my sanity …" My thoughts trailed off.

"But you'd only be getting a fraction of the dose administered to cancer patients. And you need something stronger than prednisone or azathioprine, because the peripheral neuropathy has managed to get worse, despite your being on both of these medications for the past couple of years."

I know that what the doctor is saying is true, but the leap from swallowing a few little pills with a glass of water to undergoing chemotherapy treatments seems too large to fathom at present. There must be an in between step. "Isn't there some other medication I can try? Something less severe?"

"I'm sorry. Cytoxan is the only recommendation I can make. Even Dr. Johnson agrees."

"You spoke with Dr. Johnson?"

"Yes, he has been consulting with us over the phone."

"Oh." For a few seconds, I thought Dr. Johnson, my regular rheumatologist and primary lupus doctor, had returned from his vacation. Like Dr. Scarlata, Dr. Johnson also works at the UCSF Medical Center. "Dr. Johnson has been pushing me to get on Cytoxan for a while now," I finally say.

"Yes, I know. And I was told that you were extremely reluctant to undergo treatments. But I really think that you should reconsider."

"I'll think about it."

The doctor seems to hesitate, then says, "Please take into consideration that if we don't respond to this flare-up more aggressively, the neuropathy could get a lot worse. It could spread to your limbs, or the nerves that are merely damaged now could become destroyed beyond repair. You could end up being permanently paralyzed." And with that dire prognosis, he leaves the room.

I hear a shifting and rustling of sheets on the other bed in the room. Soo Jin cries, "Don't do it, girl! They got me to do Cytoxan, and after that, I had kidney failure! I swear it was because of the chemo!"

I look at her oddly and say, "You know, another woman on dialysis told me the same thing."

"Really?"

"Yes. Her name is Tamara. I met her at Alta Bates hospital in Berkeley, right before I came here. She said that she thinks she got kidney failure because of the Cytoxan, too. She told me not to let the doctors talk me into it."

Soo Jin gestures wildly and says, "You see!? I knew it! Don't do the chemo, girl. Listen to me and Tamara! If you do it, you might end up on dialysis, too!"

This is too much to think about right now so I reach for the remote control and settle for watching the *Ricki Lake* talk show. The opening theme music is still playing and the mostly female audience is chanting, "Go Ricki! Go Ricki!

Go Ricki!"

They have increased the dose of predni-sone to 60 mg, when for the past two years I have been on 20 mg a day. At 20 mg, it felt like I was running constantly on an entire pot of coffee from the time I took my medication in the morning until I went to bed at night. I had enough en-ergy to take a full load of classes at one of the best universities in the country, par-ticipate fully in the anti-war movement on campus, be a mother to my toddler son, run a single parent household, and keep my lupus in check. But it was a plastic kind of energy, an energy that was stealing from my life's emergency fund; an energy whose days were numbered.

Multiply having loads of energy from morning until night by three, add a strong dose of crazy to the mix, and then you have the feeling of being on 60 mg of prednisone, which is where I am in this current place and time.

On the one hand, my mind is going 100 miles a minute, in loops and circles and spirals, up and down and all around, spinning into dizzying heights and making me want to run screaming through the hospital like a tormented banshee. On the other hand, I have been given anti-anxiety medication to keep my hysteria in check. I can't remember what the medication is, but I was assured of minimal side effects.

So, in a state of composed frenzy, I am embarking on my first self-imposed exercise regimen, determined to keep my cells and muscles from a state of atrophy. I somehow live with the hope that I might one day force the damaged nerve strands in my hands and feet to wake up and strive to reconnect one with the other. When they finally do – voila! – I will be healed and ready to go out dancing again.

Cane gripped tightly in my right hand, right foot up, forward, down, heel, toe, left foot shuffle, up, dangling just a bit (despite my Doc Marten combat boots), forward, straight down, clunk. I repeat this ultra slow, meticulous process again and again. My mission is ten rectangular laps around the seventh-floor corridors in a counter-clockwise direction. Ten painful, excruciating, humbling laps around an infinite floor space. But I don't dwell on it too much. I'm living moment to moment these days. It helps to keep the prednisone and the madness from taking over.

Falling into Place

I am beginning my ninth lap, and for the ninth time I jerk my head to the right as I pass by the Death Rooms on the corner. Both of the rooms look just as they have since I began my first lap: the door to the second room, the one on the right, is closed shut from prying eyes; and the first room is wide open for anyone to see. For the ninth time, I look inside the first room at the small group seated around a hospital bed, their backs facing me. I notice that the curtains have been drawn open to let in the warm sunlight, a cloudless day visible beyond the panes of glass. I glance again towards the bed before I turn the corner, but I still can't see the face of the person lying down, waiting to die.

Tuesday

The rolling cart trundles its way inside the room, inching gradually towards my end, signaling yet another blood draw. My body had already begun feeling like a human pin cushion my first day here. Two days later, with all the bruises taking shape on my arms, hands and legs, I am nervous. I am running out of places to insert needles, but I take a deep breath, brace myself and wait for the inevitable prick.

While blood is filling up a number of plastic tubes from my left hand, I ask the nurse, "Can you please take this I.V. out of my right arm?" I think she is the same nurse who initially drove it into my vein during my first hours here.

"I already told you that the doctor has to give the okay." It is, in fact, her.

"I don't see why. I should be able to

make decisions for myself. It's driving me crazy, just having this thing sticking out of my arm all day every day. It's not like I really need it."

The nurse sighs. "But you might need it. I've already explained that to you."

I sigh, too. "And I keep trying to tell you and everybody else that I should be able to make decisions regarding my own body."

The nurse won't budge. She cleans up the mess, and eventually leaves me alone to simmer in mute frustration.

From the moment the I.V. was first inserted, I have consistently asked nurses, doctors, and other staff members to please remove it. But nobody has taken me seriously. Many staff members have patiently explained to me (in a condescending manner) the same words spoken by this first nurse: that an I.V. is necessary, just in case they need to inject me with morphine for pain relief.

When I insist that I don't even want morphine, regardless of the pain, the same response from everyone (almost as if they've all rehearsed a script) is that an emergency could potentially come up, where it would be necessary to inject something into me immediately, without having to worry about taking the time and care to insert another I.V.

At one point, I sarcastically asserted to a staffer, "Well, then maybe we should all go around with I.V.'s hanging out of our arms, because an emergency could happen to anyone."

GENERIC NAME: cyclophosphamide
BRAND NAME: Cytoxan

DRUG CLASS AND MECHANISM: Cyclophosphamide is a drug that is used primarily for treating several types of cancer. In order to work, cyclophosphamide first is converted by the liver into two chemicals, acrolein and phosphoramide. Acrolein and phosphoramide are the active compounds, and they slow the growth of cancer cells by interfering with the actions of deoxyribonucleic acid (DNA) within the cancerous cells. It is, therefore, referred to as a cytotoxic drug. Unfortunately, normal cells are also affected, and this results in serious side effects. Cytoxan also suppresses the immune system and is also referred to as immunosuppressive...

SIDE EFFECTS: Side effects of cyclophosphamide include hair loss, vomiting, diarrhea, mouth sores, sterility and jaundice.

<u>Cyclophosphamide causes kidney failure,</u>

and it also may affect the heart and lungs. Cyclophosphamide suppresses production of blood cells from the bone marrow, including white blood cells (leukopenia), red blood cells (anemia), and platelets (thrombocytopenia). Leukopenia reduces the ability of the body to fight infection, thrombocytopenia impairs the ability of blood to clot, and anemia reduces the ability of blood to carry oxygen.

Cyclophosphamide also may cause inflammation of the urinary bladder with bleeding (hemorrhagic cystitis). This can result in lower abdominal pain from the bladder, problems urinating due to blood clots, and anemia due to loss of blood.
Last Editorial Review: 1/16/2000 1:01:00 PM

(http://www.medicinenet.com/cyclophosphamide/article.htm)

Falling into Place

I am on the phone long distance with my father who lives in Corpus Christi, Texas, where I was born. We are watching a tennis match as we talk, and both rooting for Serena Williams. Hearing my dad's voice keeps me calm and grounded while I wait for my first visit with my son, since my hospitalization two-and-a-half days ago.

My mom has called a few times, but does not talk for long. She hands the phone over to Jasim, instead, so that he can be reassured. When she visited yesterday she looked worn, haggard and sad. I am used to seeing a vibrant glow in her light-skinned face and green eyes. This new sunken look has me feeling guilty, for some reason. Almost as if I caused this disease to manifest.

Off in the hospital corridors nearby, I hear the nervous husky chatter of a child who has always sounded like an old blues singer. I rush to get off the phone with my dad. "Jasim is here – I've gotta go! I love you, Dad," I say.

"I love you, too, *mija*. I will be praying for you, and visualizing white light all around you."

"Thank you, Dad. Take care." Then I hang up the phone.

I am just in time to greet my mom, Herman and Jasim. My eyes are glued to Jasim's coffee-colored almond-shaped eyes that are so like my father's. I immediately check to see his reaction to seeing me lying in a hospital bed, with an I.V. sticking out of my arm. He has no memory of the first and last time I was hospitalized, back in January of 1999, when he was a month old. Now he is nearly four and I wonder what effect this will have on him. I offer a big, wide smile for

31

reassurance.

"Come here, sweetie! Mommy missed you!" I open my arms wide, he hesitates a moment, then rushes into my embrace. Despite the physical pain in my joints, I never want to let go.

My mom and Herman are extra chipper when they greet me. They have brought me a vase of flowers, and I am delighted. My mom places the vase on my nightstand, arranging the bouquet until it is just right.

"Have you eaten dinner yet?" asked Herman.

"No, not yet," I reply.

"Neither have we," says my mom. Why don't we go down to the cafeteria and get something to eat?"

I agree. I am already dressed in civilian clothes thanks to one of the nurses, but still need to put on my shoes. I can sense my mom and stepfather trying not to notice how difficult it is to tie the shoe-laces of my Doc Martens with fingers that are losing more feeling by the day. Jasim looks straight at my hands as I fumble with the laces.

Finally, I am ready. My mom has brought the wheelchair close to my bed, making sure the brakes are on. I shuffle onto the seat, and then I ask Jasim, "Would you like to ride in my lap?"

He looks frightened, but my un-wavering smile seems to offer a degree of solace, because he ends up on my lap, after all. We head out, Herman's dark brown hands pushing me, my mom walking alongside. We get in an elevator, travel down to the ground floor, and enter the noisy cafeteria.

From the moment he sat in my lap, Jasim has been continuously peeing in his pants. My clothes are starting to get wet but I pretend not to notice. Instead, I smile at everybody, participate in trivial small talk and decide what I am going to eat. We all choose our selections, and then find a table at which to sit.

The mood is light and cheerful on the surface, and I am doing my best to keep up the façade. I am drenched in my son's urine, and trying so hard not to cry. Then, as I struggle to lift a fork full of food to my mouth, I do start to cry, and before I know it, Herman and my mom are also crying, though they can't look me in the eyes.

Through the blur of tears, I notice Jasim staring off into space – a miniature astronaut in flight.

Wednesday

I have a lot of energy on my fourth day, shortly after lunchtime. This is already my second set of laps around the corridors today, and I plan to do one more set after dinner. The hospital staff must recognize the heat of determination in my eyes, for they haven't once told me to take it easy, to not push myself too hard. They haven't said much of anything to me, ever since I asked a female nurse about the Death Rooms yesterday. I wanted to know if anybody had died in them during my stay. The nurse demanded to know who had told me about them, but I pretended not to remember. Regardless, the male night nurse didn't show up to visit last night.

Cane gripped tightly in my right hand, left foot shuffle, up, dangling just a bit (even with my Docs), forward, straight down, clunk, right foot up, forward, down, heel, toe, back to the left foot, then the right, again and again and again. As always, my mission is ten laps around the seventh-floor corridors, this time in a clockwise direction. This time, not as difficult as before, though I am only on lap number one.

I am nearing the end of the first stretch, taking a deep breath in preparation for the Death Rooms I haven't passed by since this morning. Earlier, both of the doors were closed all the way, leaving me in suspense for hours. Now I can see easily into the first room, and the first thing I notice is that the curtains are pulled open and fluttering from the breeze drifting inside. There is a strong ammonia scent coming from the floors. The room is emptied of all personal content. My gaze shifts to the bed, transfixed by the crisp white sheets pulled tight at the edges, a pillow with no indentation to mar its surface. The bed just sits there in silence, as if waiting for its next occupant.

I stumble quickly by and move onto the second room. The second door is finally open, just a bit, but more than enough for me to see two people hovering over a patient. He is an old man, looking simultaneously sad and peaceful. He turns to look at me, his eyes burning into mine, a cold pale blue in winter. I shiver with the sudden chill in the corridors. I can feel Death hovering, ready to stake a claim. I quickly turn my head and shuffle away.

Soo Jin is passed out in her bed, peacefully oblivious. I am grateful to have a moment of solitude. I'm not used to sharing a room with another human being for hours on end, immersed in endless conversation. To be fair, there are plenty of quiet moments with Soo Jin, who leaves me alone with my thoughts when she senses that I need this. However, serene reflection is more attainable when she is asleep. The courteous part of me doesn't have to worry if I'm being rude.

While Soo Jin sleeps, I manage to pull myself onto the inner window ledge, so that I can better see the gorgeous view of San Francisco. The canvas before me shows a backdrop of sky the color of an early autumn blue. Here and there - and higher up - are hazy white clouds suspended in space, like smoke caught in a freeze-frame. Below is a large field of grass suitable for playing baseball or soccer. And in the middle, off in the distance, is an army of old Victorian houses and apartment buildings blinking at the mid-afternoon sun.

Xochitl M. Perales

I have disc 2 of Astor Piazzolla's *The Son of Tango – Greatest Hits* playing on my Walkman. I was never really a fan of tango music before I discovered virtuoso cellist Yo-Yo Ma's rendition of Astor Piazzolla in my mom and stepfather's music collection several years ago. The sense of joy I felt then was immense, almost as great as what I felt when I went in search of the source himself. The first time I listened to Piazzolla playing his bandoneon set to tango music was as if I had encountered my own Argentinian Pied Piper. Haunting, twisting, careening, seducing, filled with anguish, then joy and rapture, like ten thousand knives being stabbed tenderly into my heart. I was in love.

The music, along with my beautiful view of the San Francisco skyline, carries me far away from my perch on a ledge next to my hospital bed. I watch the birds flying aimlessly in the sky. I join them in their flight, soaring over rooftops, gliding by trees, flitting through clouds. Once again, the tears can't help but spill from my eyes. I never want to leave this moment.

Earlier, I came up with a mantra to see me through what I am now facing. As I sit here communing with birds, I repeat the refrain in my head: *And the sun keeps rising and setting, and the Death Rooms keep up their rotation.* In other words, life goes on.

I feel torn in two, in the middle of a tug-of-war across cultural divides. It is West versus non-West, with both teams of doctors (the rheumatologists and the neurologists) visiting me in rotation on one side, insisting that I am going to need Cytoxan chemotherapy treatment to halt

40

my current lupus flare. They keep telling me that this is the best way to ensure that no further nerve damage results. "Fingers and a foot" are one thing, and severely damaged nerves is a world away from permanent paralysis. Chemotherapy is the answer, or so they keep telling me.

On the other side stands my mother – a formidable woman who was raised in the tradition of alternative medicine, where physical ailments are cured by herbs, teas and seven-day novena candles; a mother who spent years trying to instill in me some of those same beliefs.

When I dare to at least listen to what the doctors have to say as to their reasons for pushing me to get on chemo, my mom begs me not to listen to them. "It's all a big conspiracy!" she tells me on the phone. "They just want to use you as a guinea pig for their lupus experiments and research!"

Falling into Place

When I appear unmoved by her dramatic claim, she adds, "Besides, you're in no condition to make rational choices for yourself; what with all the prednisone you're on."

I am so sick and tired of everyone trying to make decisions for me. After I get off the phone, I finally reach my limit when a nurse stops by to check my vitals right before suppertime. I kindly ask if she would please remove my I.V.

"I am not authorized to do that," she says. "You'd need to get permission from a doctor."

"Which doctor is available right now?"

"Dr. Peterson."

"Can you find him for me?"

She hesitates, "Well, I think he's

42

pretty busy with his rounds at the moment."

"I've been trying to get somebody to take this I.V. out of my arm for the past four days, and so far, nobody has listened to me. If somebody doesn't remove it soon, I swear, I will pull it out myself."

"Please don't do that! You won't be able to put pressure on your arm when you remove the I.V."

"Well, then, can you please find Dr. Peterson for me?"

"All right, I'll go get him right now," she says, and leaves the room.

A couple of hours go by, and another nurse comes in to collect yet more blood from me. I ask where the other nurse has gone. I describe what she looks like, but am told that she ended her shift and checked out for the day.

As soon as the nurse leaves, I lie down, staring at the wall for an indefinite amount of time, growing rage churning in my gut. I tamp it down, then calmly limp to the supply closet, get out some cotton balls, a bandage and alcohol, walk to the sink in plain view of my morphine-induced roommate, take off the tape holding my I.V. in place, and yank out the I.V. with my left hand.

Soo Jin shrieks as a surge of blood shoots up high into the air. She yells, "GIRL, YOU'RE CRAZY!"

AHHHH, BUT IT FEELS SO GOOD TO BE CRAZY!!

The first nurse to see me lying peacefully in my bed minus the I.V. just shakes her head at me. No one, however, says a word about it.

Thursday

I am having a major prednisone moment and I haven't been given enough anti-anxiety meds to calm me down. And now the doctor and his students have arrived, as they do every day reminding me of a cluster of ballerinas pirouetting in unison across the stage. A neurologist is at their head, only inverted and facing them, like a lioness with nothing better to do than lick accumulated dirt off her back, or interrupt my listless television watching, as the case may be. The rest of the group consists of a pack of neurology students.

They are in my room, around my borrowed bed (borrowed until I am well enough to get the hell out of here and into my queen-sized futon bed away from all distractions like blood draws beginning at the dawn and continuing regularly throughout the day, not so tasty meals and intrusive visitors barging into my room when I least expect them). They are here to participate in a class focused on my body, since this is after all not just a hospital but a teaching institution as well. Is it okay with me that I am the object of their studies? Sure. Why not? <u>My body is at their disposal.</u>

As the neurologist rambles on and on about something having to do with vasculitis, peripheral neuropathy, the left foot showing a much more pronounced foot drop than the right, the left hand showing visible weakness, the 29-year-old patient having SLE, diagnosed at age 25 during her third trimester of pregnancy, I notice that most of the medical students are young men. Lots of young men. All that firm, warm and supple flesh, those serious and penetrating eyes, the strong and pulsing hands. I imagine their hands all over my body, caressing me, running ripples up and down my thighs.

I wonder what they would have thought if they had walked in and found me lying on the hospital bed naked as a sunburst falling on midday desert plains dotted with cactus; or like a nude model waiting for community college art students who feign nonchalance while their eyes dart up, down and around the planes and crevices of the model's body, eager to paint scandalous paintings of her; the model hoping against all likelihood that each painting will rival those of Klimt, Matisse, O'Keefe, Rivera, Kahlo, among many of the Masters, resulting in paintings being dispersed across museums all over the world, awaiting the loud gasps of the most conservative and judgmental members of the subject's family.

My mind is all over the place. *All right, somebody please get me some more anti-anxiety meds!*

Falling into Place

"Yes, sweetie," I am saying to my son over the phone. "Mommy is leaving the hospital tomorrow, probably in the afternoon."

"Are we both going back home?"

"Yes, we're both going back home. Just me and you."

"And are you feeling better?"

"Yes, I'm feeling a whole lot better."

"That's good. I can't wait to see you."

"I can't wait to see you, either. I've missed you so much!"

"I've missed you, too. I'll see you tomorrow."

"Okay gorgeous. I love you."

"I love you, too, Mommy. Bye!"

It is my final night here, since all the tests that can be run have been run, and there is nothing more I can accomplish here that can't be done at home.

I am cold, so the nurse is putting another blanket on top of me. It is made from thick navy cotton, but only slightly thicker than an airplane blanket. I am just drifting off into a pleasant slumber, when all of a sudden the intercom crackles loud enough for my eardrums to twitch. A voice bellows out something incomprehensible, for the system has been broken all day.

"What the fuck?" I snap. "I'm surprised they haven't fixed it yet. Aren't they worried that all the old people will start having heart attacks?"

The nurse attending me barks out a laugh that seems to surprise even her. I like her. This one is demented. Just my style.

Falling into Place

Earlier in the night, my best friend Carmen laughed even harder at another comment I made. I was talking to her on the phone and telling her that if any of the hospital staff made an attempt to wheel me into one of the Death Rooms, all hell would break loose, because I wasn't going down without a fight! We laughed so hard it hurt.

My twisted sense of humor is starting to come back. I am glad. It helps me to cope.

Friday

I am leaving today. A couple of doctors are making one last attempt to talk me into getting on the Cytoxan chemotherapy. For now, I am against it, but not because my mother had managed to convince me with all her talk of conspiracies, or her claim that I am incapable of making my own decisions. It is because I am nervous about the possible risk of kidney failure.

The doctors are astounded that I won't automatically do their bidding. They tell me that I don't recognize the seriousness of my condition, that I am in denial.

I respond that I am a rational individual, an intelligent woman, that I take my illness seriously enough to be open to what they have to say, but that, ultimately, it is my decision to make, and they need to respect that.

I have decided that this is my body, and I am in control. For now, that is enough.

I say my goodbyes to Soo Jin and exit my hospital room for the last time, trailing in the wake of my energetic mother. She is heading left, but I turn in the opposite direction in order to get a final peek at the Death Rooms.

Both of the doors are closed all the way. From inside of the previously empty first room, the one on the left, I can hear the muffled sounds of frantic laughter bouncing off the walls, indicating that a new patient is about to die. I tilt my ear close to the door of the second room, but only silence greets me.

As I turn to leave, the door suddenly swings open, and I am faced by the surprised look of a janitor wielding a mop handle set inside of a bucket on wheels. Before he can say anything, I glance over his shoulder to see if the old blue-eyed man is still there. The room is empty.

The Hummingbird

Time past and time future
Allow but a little consciousness.
To be conscious is not to be in time
But only in time can the moment
in the rose-garden,
The moment in the arbour where
the rain beat,
The moment in the draughty church
at smokefall
Be remembered; involved with past
and future.
Only through time is conquered.

— T.S. Eliot, "Burnt Norton"

Later in September 2002
Berkeley and Albany, California

I am at the door of my apartment. My mom has driven me here from the hospital. Jasim opens the door, exploding with eagerness and joy. "Mommy! You're home!" he cries. He throws his arms around my legs, squeezing very tightly.

I flinch and struggle not to topple over. Bracing my left hand against the balcony rail seems to help. With my right hand, I hug and squeeze him back as hard as I can. I tell him, "Hello, gorgeous! I am so happy to see you!"

We head inside, my mom bringing up the rear and carrying my things. I take my shoes off just inside the entrance to my home – or, rather, my mom takes them off for me, while I support my weight against the wall and my cane, lifting first the right foot, then the left foot, leaving the left one up longer in order to have my new plastic leg brace removed after the left shoe has been set aside. I can smell the pungent aroma of garlic and olive oil sailing down the hallway. Thanks to the 60 mg of prednisone I am still on, my sense of smell is keener than ever.

Herman is cooking something in my kitchen. He had let himself into my apartment earlier with the extra set of keys I made for him and my mom. "Hi there, sweetie!" he says as he puts down a large cooking spoon. He gives me a hug while kissing me on the cheek. "Welcome back!"

"Thank you," I say.

Herman sees me looking towards the food on the stove. He tells me, "I made dinner for you and Jasim." I can see that it is spaghetti with homemade tomato sauce and turkey meatballs. Yum! My stomach growls in anticipation.

Jasim is bouncing up and down, a streak of pure happiness and excitement. There is not a single trace of fear or trauma on his face. I look at him curiously. My mom notices, and explains, "I told Jasim that you were coming home, because the doctors had given you medicine, and now you're all better!"

I cringe at the thought of what might constitute "all better" in my son's three-and-a-half-year-old brain, but decide to let it go, for now. I focus on my surroundings instead, grateful that my apartment is just as clean as I left it.

"Well, we need to get going. We have to meet some friends for dinner," says my mom. "Where should I put all your medication? Do you want it by your bed?"

"No. I'd rather have it on the counter over there," and I point to the bar space accessible from both the kitchen and the living room. "Besides, I think I'm going to sleep on the sofa-bed for awhile."

My mom puts the medication where I want it. Herman is putting his shoes on and says, "Dinner is ready, whenever you're hungry. Is there anything else you need before we go?"

Yes, I think to myself. *I need for you not to go.* I am actually surprised that they are leaving so soon. Rather than voice my concerns, however, I shake my head. "No, we're good."

"All right. We're off," says my mom. "Give Mamina a big hug," she tells Jasim. *Mamina* is the name he chose for her when he first learned to talk. She turns to me. "Bye, *mija.* I love you."

"Bye, Mom. I love you, too. Bye, Herman."

We kiss and hug, and then they are walking out the front door, across the balcony, and down the staircase. As we watch them head off down the path towards the parking lot, Jasim is holding my hand. He has a very big smile on his face.

Jasim and I have finished eating the spaghetti and turkey meatballs when we hear a knock. Carmen and her two-and-a-half-year-old daughter, Bella, are at the door. "Welcome home!" they say in unison, Bella's little bird voice adding harmony to the mix.

They come bearing gifts. Carmen carries a large clear vase filled with an assorted bouquet of flowers in shades of purple, pink, yellow, red and orange with the green making up the leaves, stems and bouquet fillers. Gripped tightly in Bella's fist is a big bundle of balloons in a rainbow of colors, including a silver one with the words "GET WELL SOON" splashed in royal blue across the front.

"Omigod. That is so sweet," I say.

"Ah, it was nothing," claims Carmen.

While the children greet each other in bubbly excitement, Carmen sets the bouquet on the floor and we hug each other real close, two balls of emotion fusing into one. I forget about the pain in my body for a long moment. We eventually break apart, and Carmen takes off her shoes and retrieves the bouquet. "Where should I put the flowers?" she asks.

"You can put them on the table."

I herd both of us with my limping shuffle down the hall and into the living room. Meanwhile, the children head off to Jasim's room to entertain themselves, balloons in tow. Carmen sets the flowers in the center of the table set against the bar space, and I decide on some jazz music to lighten the air. Five discs are chosen for my CD player, and I set the mode on random play. John Coltrane's *Blue Train* and Miles Davis's *Kind of Blue* are included in my selection. Carmen and I have an ongoing debate about who is the better jazz musician. She argues in favor of Coltrane: "His earlier pieces reflect a pure, unconscious, unadulterated genius. He is wild, frenzied, full of passionate intensity."

"Yeah, but I prefer Miles's meticulous approach. He is a master of control, brilliantly crafted synthesis, focused intention. It is a different type of genius." However, I get where Carmen is coming from. It is just a matter of personal preference that distinguishes her reasoning from mine.

Our tastes also reflect the disparities in our personalities: She is more spontaneous, and I try to fit life into a schedule;

she is a whirlwind of activity, and I function best in hermit mode; she is willing to take huge leaps into the unknown, while I weigh every possible contingency before making any move. Even in my younger, outrageously wilder years (*you have no idea!*), I usually managed to look both ways before dashing madly across life's interstate highway.

Despite our differences, and as Miles and Coltrane managed to do on a number of their albums, Carmen and I play quite well together. Our differences complement rather than detract from each other. Perhaps she is the storm, and I am the eye, and together we make chaotic structure, or structured chaos, with me preferring the latter.

The music flows out of my speakers, the notes sounding sharper due to the prednisone. I remember to be a good host and head to my wine rack for a decent bottle. I ask Carmen, "Can you open this?" and hand her a bottle opener before retrieving two sapphire blue wine glasses imported from Mexico. I probably shouldn't be drinking alcohol – a bad mix to all of the prescribed drugs in my system – but right now I need to pretend that I can function like a "normal" human being.

We sit at my small round dining table and toast my return from the hospital. We make ridiculously funny jokes and laugh in huge waves, like we always do. Our conversation is infused with philosophy (Carmen's area of expertise), politics (my preference), neighborhood gossip (we both live in the same family student housing apartment complex), parenting tips (I have one year more experience, but Carmen has read more on the subject), and everything we can think of with wine churning in our systems. Carmen pours more wine, and we continue talking until late at night.

Meanwhile, the children periodically run into the living room, then away again.

"I'm gonna get you! Tickle tickle!"

"Nooo! Ahahahaha!"

Their continuous laughter mingles like braids with the music, a sweet backdrop for adult conversation. I can hear the sound of a Scooby-Doo movie coming from Jasim's television.

"Jasim, can you please turn that down a bit?" I holler out across space, around doorframes, and above television volume levels.

He complies, but after a while, the volume mysteriously raises itself again. I shake my head and laugh with Carmen about kids being mischievous yet so adorable at their age.

I am so happy to spend time with

Carmen and Bella. My fears of returning to civilian life, of having to be responsible for another human being rather than being cared for in the hospital by others, are knocked senseless by the joy and love that are filling up my home. The medication is irrelevant, my illness doesn't matter, and the shadow of my looming future isn't pressing in on me. I'm not even thinking about the new semester of school that started without me two weeks ago. With Carmen and Bella here, everything feels bearable. I am able to find my center again. Life is good.

The following night I am sitting outside on the front terrace, smoking a cigarette. The prednisone seems to make me aware of every single moment that ticks by. I can hear the sounds of clattering dishes as someone washes them in the building facing me. Somebody else, a woman, is yelling for her child to go to bed, but there is no anger involved. A television set blares out the dialogue and audience laughter of a sitcom. A telephone rings a few times, until somebody answers it. I check to make sure I have remembered to bring my own house phone outside with me. My cell phone doesn't matter, since I rarely bother to answer it.

The smoke from my cigarette caresses the air like a lingering current. I turn my fingers slightly to form swirling patterns. Every so often, I touch the filter to my mouth, inhaling a sweet rush of nicotine into my expanding lungs. The smoke surging in and out feels like a calming breath, even as it stimulates my nerves to move faster. Even as it slowly kills me. I wonder, as I often do, what my life would have been like if I had never started smoking. What does the life of a non-smoker feel like? It's been so long I can hardly remember. I shudder at the thought of a life lived without cigarettes. I imagine that it would be like missing a limb.

The cigarette is finished, so I put it out. I do not head back inside. Jasim is fast asleep in his cheaply constructed Ikea loft bed. Everything is clean. The dishes are washed. There is nothing to attend to inside the apartment, so I remain seated in my chair. I am looking at the stars, marveling at the infinite universe. There is a slight rustle in the trees. The breeze caresses my face like a whisper being chased through the dark. I can smell a touch of autumn in the air, though the weather is still quite warm in Berkeley.

My mental perambulation is suddenly pierced in mid-stride and I hesitate. A melodious sound is penetrating the shroud of my meditation. It is coming from far away, and I yearn to hear it up close. Level by level, my mind emerges from the clouds. I slowly come back into myself, like a woman waking up from a coma. I realize that the music is coming from nearby, directly in my line of vision. I am surprised to find that it is my neighbor, P.J., playing her flute from the apartment building in front of mine.

I lean my head back against the wall and let my mind merge with the music. I can feel the notes echoing inside the caverns of my eardrums. They go down further to swim through my bloodstream, dancing softly on organs and embracing cell walls. A trembling is taking hold of me, like volcanic matter on the verge of eruption.

The trembling has spread. It has reached outside of me, reverberating in the Earth. I can feel the ground shaking in time to my own bodily jolts. Then it is as if we are one, the Earth, myself, and P.J.'s magical flute. There is an echo ringing inside my ears. An enormous shiver washes over me in one great big swallow. Then there is stillness. I am gripping the edges of my chair as tightly as I can, and yet I feel no physical sensation taking place. Rather, I am glorying in the unreality of this moment.

After an eternity, the otherworldly spell begins to wear off. I am thinking to myself, *Oh my God! This is the power that gives blind people the ability to see, and the crippled the ability to get up out of their wheelchairs and walk!* This leads me to wonder if I will regain feeling in my peripheral nerves right now, this second. Then a tiny glimmer of doubt appears on my horizon, the blind faith is gone, and I know I will not walk on water just yet. I flex my hands and feet just to be sure.

Falling into Place

Nothing.

The next day, Carmen, Bella, Jasim and I are on our way to a special event for UC Berkeley student parents and their families. It is taking place at University Village, a large family student housing complex located in the small community of Albany. I used to live there, before I transferred to my current residence within the Smyth Fernwald complex in Berkeley. Smyth is closer to campus, but more importantly, there is no mold growing inside the walls, making my son sick all the time. There's also the added bonus of having Carmen and Bella close by.

It is the beginning of the 2002-03 school year. The event we are going to is to welcome new families into the community, but also to provide entertainment for those of us who have been student parents longer. I think of it as a pre-reward for all of the spouses and children who will soon have to suffer through the insane roller coaster ride of midterms, papers and finals, along with the family members actually attending school. The veteran students with children have begun to notice the increase in bed wettings and thumb suckings that take place in our households every time a new semester starts. My own child has reverted to sucking on a couple of pacifiers he somehow managed to hide when I threw the rest away. After my recent hospital stay, it is easy to allow my boy his solace.

Carmen is driving our little group of four to the event. We arrive on the grounds, and Carmen manages to find a parking space close to all of the activity. I put on my floppy straw hat and heft my aching limbs out of the car, utilizing my cane for support. After Carmen un-buckles the kids from their car seats, they scramble out onto the asphalt and hurry to the sidewalk's safety zone.

"Bella, Jasim, do you guys need to use the bathroom?" Carmen asks. There is a bathroom in the nearby community center.

"I do, I do," chimes Bella.

"I'm okay," says Jasim in a raspy voice.

Carmen glances at my cane and says, "Do you want to wait for us here?"

"Why don't we just meet up later? We can reach each other on our cell phones. That way, you can visit with some of your other friends."

"All right. Sounds like a plan. See you guys in a little bit." Carmen and Bella turn to leave.

I take a moment to gather my bearings. My mind, full of prednisone, is swirling with the overlapping noise of adults conversing, babies crying, children laughing, cars honking, and parents yelling at their kids to stay close where they can see them. I inhale, then exhale, to filter out the commotion. To unleash my inner calm.

"Okay, Jasim. What would you like to do first?" I ask.

Jasim is shifting his gaze all over the place. He is overcome with all of the sights and sounds around us. He wants to do everything at once: eat hot dogs, visit the petting zoo, ride a pony, bounce up and down in the huge blow-up jumper, skate down the water slide. I want to accommodate his short attention span, but I can only go so fast.

At first, he is somewhat patient with my slow progress. But after a while, Jasim grabs my left hand, the one not holding onto the cane for balance. "Come on,

Mommy! Hurry! Let's go!" He is aiming for the water slide.

"Wait, sweetie! Not so fast!" I re-adjust my cane in my right hand. I have more feeling in this hand than my left, but it is still hard to grip the cane securely.

Jasim sees me struggling with the cane. Quick as lightning, his mood turns to anger. "No!" he yells. "You don't need the cane! You're all better now!" He knocks the cane out of my hand. I lose my balance and fall to the ground.

I reach over to retrieve the cane, but Jasim is trying to yank it away from me. We are in the midst of a tug-of-war. Jasim is screaming at me, tears pouring down his face. Someone grabs hold of him as the cane clatters to the ground once more. Another person helps me up, and someone else hands my cane back to me. I notice a familiar woman standing right next to me. She is the resident social worker for student parents. "Are you okay?" she asks. I break down sobbing in her arms.

Behind me, I can hear Jasim shrieking all of his fears out into the exosphere.

Later that night. I have just finished reading Jasim his favorite book, *No, David!* by David Shannon. "So you see, even David does things he is not supposed to do," I explain. "And in the end, he gets a great big hug from his mommy." I demonstrate by giving Jasim the biggest hug I can manage. He responds with a slight hug.

I release my arms and look into his eyes. They are shadowed and loaded with sorrow. There might even be guilt left over from the earlier cane incident, despite my best efforts in choosing the right story to read. I pull out his pacifier and aim to kiss him on his lips while holding his gaze, but he turns his head slightly when I am almost there, so I settle for kissing his right cheek instead. I say, "Goodnight, gorgeous," put the pacifier back in his mouth and tuck the blankets securely around him. One more kiss on his forehead and I am turning his night-light on, his overhead light off, and heading out the door. I leave it halfway open.

I am gone less than fifteen minutes when I hear Jasim yelling in his sleep. I rush inside his room and squint in the darkness. I can see the pacifier has fallen out of his mouth and that he is agitated. Tossing and turning. Kicking the blankets off. Reaching his hands everywhere in desperation, though he is not awake.

I find the pacifier for him and plop the nipple side into his mouth. I notice that he settles down immediately. I sit next to him on the edge of the bed, caressing his soft brown curls that are damp from fear. I make shhh-ing noises and say, "It's all right, sweetie. Mommy's here. And I love you very much."

He is breathing deeply through his nostrils and making loud sucking noises against the pacifier. There is still sweat on his brow, but his facial muscles appear more relaxed. His body has managed relative stillness, except for the unconscious twitch of his left hand to touch his left ear. His hand repeats the motion again and again, an isolated worker in an assembly line of trauma. I reach out to grab his hand, to hold it still. I kiss his wrist lightly, and his body shudders in response.

A day later, and I am driving again. It is

mid-morning, but there is plenty of traffic on the streets of Berkeley. The further I drive from campus, the fewer pedestrians there are clogging up the sidewalks and intersections. It is a beautiful day, clear of fog and full of sunshine. But fortunately for me, who does not love hot weather, there is a cool breeze blowing through my slightly lowered windows. And though my skin doesn't take well to sunlight, there is plenty of shade inside the car.

Early this morning I asked Carmen to take Jasim to the pre-school he shares with Bella. I could have kept him home with me, but decided it was better to give him back his normal routine. Having him in pre-school also gives me the chance to develop my own routine, and to relearn autonomy. I want to minimize the favors that Carmen, my mom and Herman will undoubtedly do for me as my body slowly heals. I hate being a

burden. I also need to prepare for my return to school, hopefully by the end of
the week. Above all, I want to give Jasim
another bundle of hope to cling onto.

I approach a red light and prepare
to slow down. It is strange pressing into
the clutch with a foot that feels almost
nothing. I am wearing my new leg brace
in order to walk around more easily, and
it also helps with the driving. The plastic hardness embracing my foot under-
neath offers the force I need to help push
the clutch down. With each downward
thrust, the top part of the brace, strapped
in Velcro just below my kneecap, presses
into skin with far more feeling than the
bottom part of my leg, the part closer to
my foot drop. Without this movement of
the brace higher up, along with the feeling it generates, it would be very difficult
for me to know whether or not the clutch
was pushed in all the way. Perhaps if I

tilted my head to look down each time, but then, who would pay attention to the road for me?

The light turns green, and I ease into first gear.

Two days later, it is the eve of my return to school, and Jasim is throwing a huge temper tantrum. He is furious that he can't have his way. I am trying to reason with him, but he just won't budge. Finally, I reach the edge of my limit. In barely controlled tones, I say, "Go to your room!"

"No!"

I take a very deep breath. "I, said, go, to your room!" He still won't budge, so I add, "Right now!!"

"NO!!!"

Something inside of me snaps.

"THAT'S IT!!! I'VE HAD IT!!!" I grab his left shoulder firmly. Oddly enough, as I look into his eyes, a spear of compassion hits me. Mingled with my anger at his rebellion, my love for him propels me to continue what I have started. He kicks and screams at me, flailing his arms in agitation, so I half carry, half drag him to his room. I somehow manage this feat, despite the loss of feeling in my hands, and without tripping over my lame left foot that isn't wearing the plastic leg brace inside the apartment.

I get him to his room and throw him inside and halfway across the floor. "STAY IN YOUR ROOM UNTIL I SAY YOU CAN COME OUT!!!" I slam the door shut.

I can hear Jasim's loud gushing sobs while I stand outside of his door for what feels like an unbearable span of time. I want so badly to rush inside and gather him tenderly into my arms. Instead, I hold back. *It's for his own good,* I assure myself. Somehow, instinctively, I know that Jasim needs this. He needs to know that his mommy is strong enough to set boundaries. This is a test, however unconscious, and I am determined to pass with soaring colors. I am determined to set things right.

I block out the sound of Jasim's anguish and limp to the kitchen to wash the dishes.

A couple of weeks have gone by, and I am getting an acupuncture treatment. My acupuncturist, Robert, has become a necessary presence in my life. He was passed down from two friends of the family, to my mom, and finally, to me. I initially went to see him for a few weeks when I was twenty-one, hoping that he could do something about my right knee which had swollen to the size of a softball. I didn't yet know that I had lupus, and the most that Robert could tell me was that I seemed to have some sort of virus, and not the rheumatoid arthritis that everyone else thought I had. Regardless, his acupuncture treatments did manage to relieve the swelling and related pain.

I started seeing Robert again, on and off, after my lupus diagnosis when I was twenty-five. At first, I was afraid to mix the Chinese herbs he gave me with the meds I was taking for my lupus. But his experience with Western medicine took care of any reluctance on my part. He had been a pharmacist until one day he heard a report about acupuncture on National Public Radio, which changed his whole perspective on healing, and he switched to Eastern practices. Having lived on both sides of the medical divide, Robert seemed like the ideal candidate to help guide me through alternative forms of healing.

After this recent flare-up and hospitalization, I now come to Robert for acupuncture treatments three times a week. This is my second visit of the week, and I am in one of Robert's small, compact rooms. It is early afternoon. I am lying down on my back, the hard, flat surface of the table bed lengthening my spine. I am doing my best to relax, a difficult feat given all the prednisone in my bloodstream. However, my rheumatologist, Dr. Johnson, recently allowed for a decrease in dosage to 50 mg, a significant improvement from the previously prescribed 60 mg. And yet it is not enough to counter the onslaught of thought patterns coalescing in my mind like unbroken loops from morning until night, every single day. I am impatient to keep going lower and lower, to continue reducing the dosage until these thoughts, like swarming bees, are repelled.

My greatest wish is to get off the prednisone completely, and Robert promises to help me achieve this goal. "But it will be a slow process," he says after taking out the last needle. "In order to get off of Western medicine, you would first need to balance your mind, body, spirit and heart. This would involve a very strict detox diet." He starts enumerating on his fingers, "many acupuncture sessions, Chinese herbs that I can give you myself, and as little stress in your life as possible." He pauses for emphasis, looks me squarely in the eyes, and says, "It will also take patience on your part, because this is going to take a while."

"How long is a while?"

"I can't really say."

"Are we talking weeks? Months? Years?"

"Why don't we just take things one day at a time."

I can feel panic mounting an offensive attack. My breathing is quicker, and I am shifting restlessly on the table bed. I think about pulling my hair out and screaming, *But I want off the prednisone right now!!* Ironically, it is the prednisone itself that makes me so desperate to get off of it.

"Try to keep still," Robert says. He is getting ready to insert needles into various pressure points throughout my body. They are inserted one by one, until suddenly there are needles galore sticking out of my ears, arms, hands, knees, feet. At first there is slight pain, a bit awkward, but not too bad. When Robert twists a few needles, different parts of my body jolt as though being given minor electric shock treatments. The pain is a bit sharper in these instances. Then it is over, and he positions a lamp to shine directly above my left knee. A large red bulb emits warmth, and I am content enough to relax. My bones melt into liquid. The needles are forgotten. Tears slide down by cheekbones before I drift into a soft unconsciousness.

Before I know it, Robert's pale smooth hands are deftly removing the needles and placing them on a paper towel lying on the counter. I can see his progress reflected in a warped manner off of his round wire frame spectacles. Behind the reflection, his light blue eyes look at me with serious intent. I glance up and notice strands of grayish hair hanging diagonally across his forehead.

When he takes the last needle out, he says, "There we are. All done. Do you feel better now?"

"Yes. I'm a lot more relaxed."

"Good. I'll see you in a couple of days."

"What about the detox diet you wanted me to go on?"

"Let's talk about that later, after your body has adjusted to the 50 mg of prednisone." He must notice the slight agitation that I too can feel crinkling into my brow, because he adds, "Look at what you've already accomplished: You've decreased from 60 to 50 mg of prednisone, you're driving again, you're back in school."

"I know, I know. You're right. It's just that I want my life to be back to normal."

"And it will be. Just be patient. Remember, one step at a time."

Later in the day, I climb the steps to my second-floor apartment. My left foot is dragging more than usual, but I finally reach the landing. Jasim is already waiting in our small porch area in front of the door, twirling around, tapping his feet, and humming a tune he probably learned in pre-school. As usual, he is a cyclone of hyperactivity, flitting from one activity to the next. When I reach his side, I fumble with my keys for the right one and insert it into the lock. As I turn the doorknob, Jasim positions himself above the three large empty water bottles that are lined up on the left side of our front porch, waiting to be traded for full ones when the Arrowhead delivery person makes his or her next scheduled delivery.

I wait for the inevitable "Boom boom boom" of Jasim hitting the water bottles in order, from left to right, just as he always does when we arrive home.

When we leave, he does it in reverse, "Boom boom boom" from right to left, always in that order, one at a time, whether the bottles are full or empty. The only variation in either pattern occurs when there are less than three bottles, in which case Jasim is forced to make adjustments. He doesn't seem to mind when there are one or two bottles, but when there are none I can see the tension mounting by the way he starts grabbing his left ear in a repetitive ticking motion, or by the rapid movement of his eyes that appear to be searching for something that is lost. In those moments, it's as if his world is off-kilter.

Luckily for him, this is not one of those moments. "Boom boom boom," go the empty water bottles when Jasim hits them. The prednisone makes me flinch a little, but I'm relieved that for now at least, my son's world is spinning as it should be, from left to right.

The next day, I am sitting on my front deck once again, smoking a cigarette. It is mid-afternoon. The sky is clear and blue, the air is perfect, the sun is not hitting me directly. Most of the residents are away, either at work or at school. I am, for the most part, alone.

I take a drag of my cigarette, and a hummingbird flies into my line of vision, just a short distance away. It floats blurrily amidst the trees lining the second story deck that runs along my building. These days, I am used to hummingbirds. They seem to follow me wherever I go. They appear out of nowhere, shimmering cheerleaders to my self-prescribed physical therapy sessions, as I endeavor relearning to walk up and down and all around my apartment complex. I see them just about every time I step outside to have a cigarette, or as I make my way to and from the parking lot. They sometimes visit me on campus, but it is harder to notice them when my mind is set on struggling to put one foot in front of the other to get to class.

The hummingbird before me is now perching on a leaf. Somehow, it is managing to remain perfectly still for an indefinite span of time. Ten seconds pass by, perhaps thirty. Who knows? I am frozen in time and watching, holding my breath, not even allowing myself to contemplate the significance of the moment. I just want to be completely *in* the moment. The time for reflection will come later.

The hummingbird is fluttering in its usual pattern once more, quick as lightning and blurry as fog. It has landed

again on a leaf (the same leaf?), and yet
again becomes totally still for what feels
like a long while. I can see the hummingbird so clearly, the long, needle-like beak,
the observant eyes, the brown and gray
hues of feathers. There is no blur of motion to play tricks on my senses. I can
see the hummingbird in all of its glory,
remaining absolutely, utterly still.

Suddenly, it appears as though
the hummingbird is looking me in the
eyes. It is flying straight towards me! It
stops but a few inches away, does a little
dancing motion in front of me, and then
slightly above. The dance continues, first
to one side, then the other, and then up
and down, kind of like a cross. Oh! But
now he is flying with superhuman speed
back into the tree branches!

I am reeling from the ethereal qual-
ity to the air, left behind in sparkling
flashes as the hummingbird made its swift

exit. When I am able to start thinking coherently once more, I ask myself, *Can hummingbirds even be still for that long?*

My own reply is that if I can be still long enough to even capture this moment in a snapshot while on 50 mg of prednisone, then of course hummingbirds can be still for that long.

GENERIC NAME: Prednisone
BRAND NAME: Deltasone, Orasone, Prednicen-M, Liquid Pred

DRUG CLASS AND MECHANISM: Prednisone is an oral, synthetic (man-made) corticosteroid used for suppressing the immune system and inflammation. It has effects similar to other corticosteroids such as triamcinolone (Kenacort), methylprednisolone (Medrol), prednisolone (Prelone) and dexamethasone (Decadron). These synthetic corticosteroids mimic the action of cortisol (hydrocortisone), the naturally-occurring corticosteroid produced in the body by the adrenal glands. Corticosteroids have many effects on the body, but they most often are used for their potent anti-inflammatory effects, particularly in those diseases and conditions in which the immune system plays an important role. Such conditions include arthritis, colitis, asthma, bronchitis, certain skin rashes, and allergic or inflammatory conditions of the nose and eyes. Prednisone is inactive in the body and, in order to be effective, first must be converted to prednisolone by enzymes in the liver. Therefore, prednisone may not work as effectively in people with liver disease whose ability to convert prednisone to prednisolone is impaired…

SIDE EFFECTS: Side effects of prednisone

and other corticosteroids range from mild annoyances to serious, irreversible damage, and they occur more frequently with higher doses and more prolonged treatment. Side effects include retention of sodium (salt) and fluid, weight gain, high blood pressure, loss of potassium, headache and muscle weakness. Prednisone also causes puffiness of the face (moon face), growth of facial hair, thinning and easy bruising of the skin, impaired wound healing, glaucoma, cataracts, ulcers in the stomach and abdomen, worsening of diabetes, irregular menses, rounding of the upper back ("buffalo hump"), obesity, retardation of growth in children, convulsions, and _psychiatric disturbances. The psychiatric disturbances include depression, euphoria, insomnia, mood swings, personality changes, and even psychotic behavior._

(https://www.medicinenet.com/prednisone/
article.htm)

Soon after the hummingbird episode, I rush inside to call Lata and Ruth. They are the two friends of the family who first discovered Robert, the acupuncturist. I leave a message about the hummingbird when they don't answer, but I am not there to pick up the phone when they call back. I listen to Lata's message, her South Asian accent, "It's such a beautiful thing, the experience you had today. Ruth was reminding me that a hummingbird represents transformation. And the other thing that struck me after hearing your message was that a hummingbird's heartbeat is 240 beats a minute. And I think that what you said about being still while on prednisone is very relevant, because I think that part of what you experienced was the possibility of being still in the midst of this kind of rapid internal movement, and I've never seen a hummingbird do what you experienced today. So it was a really special blessing and a visitation. I'm so glad you called and told us about it."

For the next few days, I am walking around surrounded by light, infused with a grace and beauty that seeps through my pores, enveloping me in a warm, bright halo. I don't even blink when the hummingbirds continue with their visits, appearing out of mist and fluttering by my side, my sweet little guardian angels.

Even Carmen notices. On the last Sunday in September, when I casually explain to a neighbor that hummingbirds follow me everywhere, the neighbor humors me by nodding when expected. Yet her clenched smile let me know that she thought I belonged in a mental ward. Carmen backs me up, saying, "It's true.

They're around her all the time."

As Carmen is my witness, I know I am blessed.

The next day, Jasim is in pre-school, and I am reading some densely worded articles within the compiled Course Reader for the Peace Theory class I am enrolled in for the second time. A year ago, when I took it the first time, I dropped the class halfway through the semester. It was during the weeks following September 11, 2001 and I was too involved with political activism to concentrate on a theory class.

I am flipping through the pages of the Reader until I reach the portion we have been assigned to read for the week. On the first page is a T.S. Eliot poem entitled "Burnt Norton". I am amazed that despite its complexly philosophical musings concerning the relationship between time and space, and regardless of the poem's abstract references to teachings from Christianity, Hinduism and Buddhism about things like redemption, consciousness and eternity (ideas generally beyond my scope of knowledge), the poem makes absolute sense to me; especially the section about past and future time, consciousness, and conquering time through time itself. I feel like I have gone through this experience: <u>I have managed to fracture time while on a drug that constantly pushes me outside of time.</u>

A revelation blossoms in my mind. I think about some of the recent moments in my life: feeling the Earth stop spinning on its axis in time to the notes coming from P.J.'s flute; Robert's advice about taking things *one step at a time*; the visit from my special hummingbird; the confirmation from Lata, Ruth and Car-

100

men; and now the Eliot poem coming into my life at this precise moment.

I feel like the pieces are falling into place. My heart is open. Life is beautiful. I am on a road called Catharsis.

Later that night, I wish I could share some of my newfound revelations with Jasim. But he is occupied (and too young besides). It is almost his bedtime, and I am standing outside of his doorway, watching him. He is squatting on his haunches, rocking back and forth, and singing a song. It is the Alphabet song, the one we all learn as children.

"...H-I-J-K-LMNO-P.   Q-R-S. T-U-V. W-X. Y and Z. Now I know my A-B-C's. Next time won't you sing with me." He sings perfectly; the cadence, tone and sound all effortlessly pitched.

Falling into Place

I clap my hands and say, "Yay! Good job, Jasim!"

He doesn't acknowledge my presence or my praise, and begins the song again: "A-B-C-D-E-F-G." When he is all done with this round, he sings the tune in its entirety yet again. And again a fourth time.

On the fifth round, I can no longer pretend that this is normal behavior. Something is definitely not right. I walk over to him and interrupt with, "Okay, Jasim. That's enough. One more time, and that's it."

I can't grab his visual attention with a stare at close range, but he does pause for a few seconds in the middle of the song. Then he continues where he left off: "Q-R-S. T-U-V. W-X. Y and Z. Now I know my A-B-C's. Next time won't you sing with me."

I am scared when he starts the song

a sixth time, all the way through until the last note. But then the singing is done, and he doesn't begin the dreaded seventh round. Instead, he is looking at some point in front of him, squatting at attention, as if awaiting further command.

Before issuing my next set of instructions, I take a moment to note that Jasim has managed the unattainable. He is perfectly still.

Falling into Place

Welcome to Rock Bottom

The first half of January 2003
Berkeley, California

A moment of panic bursts like a flower inside my chest cavity. The lights are out. I am in a strange place. I don't want to be here, in a room full of sad, old women, entrenched in an atmosphere of no hope. I am beyond no hope. Instead, I want to die.

"I want to die!" I yell into space. "Please, God!" (Or Whomever.) "Let me die!"

I am lying in a hospital bed inside a geriatric ward. I am on my back, staring at the darkness stretching above me. I want to cry, but my eyes are incapable of producing tears. Wrenching pain pours out, immobilizing me. It is a torrid grief, made crisp by the smells of aging flesh and bed sheets drenched in urine-tinged sweat that lingers over the room. The bodies of my three roommates rustle and shift, silent witnesses to my anguish.

After a while, a woman in the bed to my left reaches for the intercom.

"Can I help you?" a male voice asks on the other end.

"I am having heart palpitations," says the woman in a worried voice. "I need you to call my daughter for me."

"Hang on, ma'am. I'll send some-one right over to check on you."

Some time passes before a doctor turns on the main light switch and enters the room. He walks directly towards the woman with heart palpitations and asks, "What seems to be the problem?"

"I think I might be having a heart attack," she says.

I think you might be suffering from

a broken heart, I speculate. Who can blame her, in this heartless place, with no friends or family to help soothe fears of imminent death — for every patient here seems long past the age of seventy. Everyone except for me, but I guess my health condition gives me certain privileges.

The broken-hearted woman is pronounced to be fine by the doctor, but still wants her daughter to know what's going on. After someone hands her a cordless phone, I can hear everything she is saying to her daughter. At one point, she asks, "Do you promise to come see me tomorrow?" There is a short monologue on the other end, then she says, "Yes, I'll go back to sleep now. I hope to see you tomorrow. Good night." She hangs up the phone and sits on the side of her bed, facing me, but looking at the floor.

Someone turns out the lights. Another wave of panic hits me. "I want to die!" I call out to no one in particular. Or perhaps I am making an appeal to the woman with the broken heart. Whatever my intention, she answers me.

"What's wrong?" she asks.

"I don't want to live anymore! Please, God! Please, let me die!"

The woman doesn't say anything. I can hear her soft breathing.

My pitiful words are a comforting refrain in my head. I let them try to rock me to sleep, though my eyes are still open, staring at the darkness once more.

The old woman remains seated on her bed, yearning for her daughter, perhaps as my son is yearning for me from somewhere. I don't think about that, and close my eyes.

It is likely the next day when I ask, "Can

I please have some privacy?"

The male attendant is seated in a chair next to me, watching me hunched over in the bathtub, my arms trying to cover my naked body from round brown eyes that are set below a prominent forehead.

"I'm sorry," he says in an accent that brings Ethiopia or Eritrea to mind, "but I was instructed not to leave you by yourself. You have been listed as a suicide threat."

"Then can I get a female attendant to watch over me while I bathe?" I am thinking about the big woman who undressed me and helped get me out of the wheelchair and into the tub.

"Unfortunately, there are no female personnel available right now."

"Can I at least have the curtain closed, then?"

The attendant hesitates, "I am not

sure if that is the best idea."

I look at him with earnest eyes, and plead, "What if I continue making some kind of noise, so that you know I haven't drowned myself? I could even hum for you."

"Well, I guess that would be acceptable," he says. "But don't stop humming, or I shall be forced to keep the curtain open again. And don't let the water fill up too high."

"I won't."

I stretch out my slender legs in almost parallel lines, while a made-up tune seeps out from between my lips. Redundant feet are flapping beneath an onslaught of warm water, willowy arms floating along my sides. My bodily curves are faint, taking a backseat to the sharp bones sticking out at intermittent angles near the vicinity of my hips and along my ribcage. Clearly noticeable are my breasts jutting out from the water, with large, hardened nipples like unblinking eyes, staring morosely at the ceiling.

I lie there humming, imagining my lungs being drowned with mercy. *Do I have it in me to hold my breath under water long enough to die? Would my life really flash before my eyes in the final moments, as in movies?*

"Is it time to turn the tap off?" asks the attendant.

"Yes, thank you. The water is starting to get high."

He opens the curtain to turn off the single knob. I try to cover my body again, keeping my legs straight, with my lifeless left hand settled over my vaginal region, and my right arm bent and hiding my nipples from view. I am humming softly once more, and plotting ways to end this bleak existence I no longer want. I picture this very same male attendant gasping in horror over my blue, lifeless corpse bobbing like a giant coreless apple in the tub. I manage to keep a bitter laugh in check, barely aware that the curtain is closing me from view, and my imagined performance, fading to black.

Time passes without my noticing. I am not aware of my surroundings.

"Miss, you need to come out and join everyone in the dining hall for dinner," says some random attendant whose voice I would not recognize if I cared enough to try. "You can't stay in here forever."

I make no attempt to answer, no move to face her. I continue looking at a point on the wall before me, my back guarding against the frustrated pleas this woman is throwing at me. I hear her words from a great distance, muffled by the endless stretch of tunnel standing between them and my unwillingness to collapse my soul back into its material shell. I like the view from where I am now just fine, with its consoling whispers and honeycombed trails. I don't want to return to that other world, the one that left me in shreds.

"You really should get out of this bed," she continues. "The only way you'll get better is if you exercise your body. Otherwise, your muscles could atrophy, and your nerves might not stand a chance of regenerating."

There is still no response from me, because I have stopped believing in miracles. I just want to be left by myself in this private room that was somehow given to me yesterday (or was it today?) and be alone with joyous thoughts of leaving this ugly world.

112

Xochitl M. Perales

I want this annoying presence at my back to leave me in peace.

When she threatens to remain until I have agreed to get out of bed and eat in the dining hall, my mind calls me back for one more act. *Make her go away!* it pleads. *Think of something quick!*

"My leg is hurting really bad," I tell her. "I'm in too much pain to get out of bed."

"Would you like me to get the doctor?"

"Yes, that would be good."

Some time later a doctor arrives. "I hear that you are feeling a lot of pain in one of your legs," he begins.

I turn around to face him, nod my head and say, "Yes."

"Which leg is it?"

"The right leg."

"Last time you said it was the left leg." His tone is skeptical.

113

"They both hurt!" I rush to clarify. "It's just that the right leg hurts more."

"Hmmm. Well, I guess I'll order another round of Dilaudid for you. Hopefully that will ease the pain."

"Yes, I'm sure it will. Thank you."

I am alone again, grateful to resume my fantasies about killing myself. I imagine grabbing the pen in the nightstand and slitting my wrists into bright red gashes of gore. I can see the cartilage springing forth, the blood spilling out in miniature waterfalls onto the pristine hospital floor, the life draining out of me in rivulets. Unfortunately, the function in both of my hands is virtually nonexistent, so I discard that plan quickly, even as I linger over the image of sliced open and bloodied wrists in my head.

Fortunately for those who might not want to see me dead in such a gruesome fashion (if I were but capable), the nurse arrives with my Dilaudid injection. I watch her plunge the needle into my arm, and feel the medicine surge through my cells.

Now that I have learned to stop fighting it, it doesn't take long for the Dilaudid to work its magic. It becomes a balm to my bleak life, draining away the loud gust of panic and high dose of prednisone I feel whenever I reunite my mind with my soul long enough to communicate with hospital personnel. There is nothing to worry about when Dilaudid is flowing through my nerve endings. I think to myself, *Life ain't so bad.*

"Why hello, there! Who do we have here?" wonders a lean, thriving woman with gray hair, leathery beige skin and light blue eyes. When I don't answer right away, she asks, "What is your name, honey?"

"Xochi."

"Xochi! What a lovely name! I'm Evelyn."

"Nice to meet you."

The male attendant pushing my wheelchair brings me closer to the long dining hall where dinner is being served. This is the first time I have been forced to join the world of the living in this place, to leave the comfort of my own private hell, on what I believe to be my fourth or fifth day.

Evelyn notices the attendant opening a container of apple juice for me. When he begins cutting my boneless chicken into bite-sized pieces, she tells him, "Here, I'll do that for you, so that you can go on about your duties." Then she looks at me and asks, "Do you mind?"

"No, that'll be fine," I say, not quite

looking her in the eyes.

"So, what brings you here to our happy little abode?" she asks, lifting a shaking fork of chicken to my mouth, and waiting for me to take a bite.

After chewing deliberately for a few seconds, I say, "I have lupus, and am going through a really bad flare-up right now."

"Lupus! That's a crummy illness to have for someone so young!"

"Yeah, it really sucks," I sigh.

"Well, I have Parkinson's, but I got it when I was a lot older than you."

"That's too bad." I don't know what else to say.

"Are you from around here?" she asks.

"I'm originally from Corpus Christi, Texas, but I've lived all over. I've been living in the Bay Area since '92."

"I'm from Pasadena, and stay in a

nursing home out there. But then I started flipping out about a week ago, and my daughter, who lives in Berkeley, wanted to have me committed here, so I could be closer to her."

"Oh."

"Do you have any kids?"

"Yes. I have a four-year-old son. His name is Jasim."

Evelyn waits for me to say more, and when I don't, she asks, "So, why are you in here, with a bunch of crazy old people, instead of another loony ward with people your own age, or upstairs in physical therapy?"

I decide to be honest. "My family was afraid that I'd try to kill myself, so they wanted me to check myself into a psychiatric ward. I couldn't go to one with people my own age, because they didn't have medical doctors on call 24-hours-a-day like they do here."

"Ah, I see." With a twitching hand, she feeds me another bite of food, this time a forkful of peas and mashed potatoes mixed together. She asks, "So, do you feel like killing yourself right now?"

I am startled by her bluntness. For some reason, though, I feel no qualms about sharing my darkest secrets with her. "Yes. Unfortunately, I have no feeling in my hands, and can't do anything about it."

A laugh explodes from Evelyn's throat. "Life sure is funny that way," she says. "Well, you might not be happy that you're still alive, but I am. If you had managed to kill yourself before now, I wouldn't have been able to meet you."

I feel a slight warm glow touching my insides, but say nothing. I take another bite of chicken, chewing carefully, feeling the needed calories nourish my frail body.

Falling into Place

Evelyn brings the apple juice to my lips, and I take a couple of large gulps. She uses a napkin to wipe away the dribble that has run down my chin. "When we're done here, would you like to take a stroll with me around our illustrious grounds?" she asks with a flourishing sweep of her arm and an animated smile on her face.

I return the smile in a smaller dose, saying, "Yes, that would be nice."

I feel the anxiety choking me with an iron fist. I don't want to be here anymore, in this worthless shell of a body that can do nothing but sit or lie down. I don't want to live anymore. *Oh, God, please let me die!*

I'm not sure what day it is, but I know that it's nighttime, because dinner ended not too long ago. I am seated all alone on one of the lumpy couches in front of the communal TV. Most of the patients have gone to bed, including Evelyn. But I have never been able to break the habit of staying up late, not even when I became a parent and had to get up early in the morning to take my son to school.

Thinking about Jasim brings on another wave of panic. A nurse walks towards me. She has an infusion of Dilaudid ready for me, and she plunges it steadily into my right arm. *I wonder how she knows that I need this?* I immediately feel better, long before the medicine has really had a chance to take effect.

An elderly black lady comes over and volunteers to spoon-feed me chocolate pudding at this late hour. She manages to convince one of the night staff to bring me a container, even though the kitchen has been locked up for the night. She offers up each spoonful the way a mother might feed her one-year-old child, only without all of the airplane fanfare.

After every few bites, the lady takes the time to wipe my mouth clean of chocolate remnants, dabbing at the corners in birdlike gestures. She tells me, "What a sweet girl you are."

The pudding is all gone, and the lady has wandered off somewhere. I am stretched out on the couch, watching TV by myself again. I get an attendant to flip through the channels for me, wishing there was something to watch besides more September 11th protests on the local news. I settle on an old episode of *The Simpsons*, the one where Lisa is in the sky, but as a cartoon member of The Beatles points out, with no diamonds.

An old white man wearing thick,

black-framed glasses stops by my couch. He asks me, "Are you cold?"

"I'm okay."

He ignores me, saying, "Here, let me get you a warm blanket." He reaches inside a large heating unit next to the television, filled with thinly woven blankets. Before he can drape it over me, the puddling lady snatches it out of his hands.

"I was just trying to cover the girl with it," the man insists.

"I'll do it for her," the lady snaps.

The man starts to walk off in a huff, but I call out a thank-you before he leaves.

The blanket falls over my body in a smooth flap. The lady tucks it around my edges with her dark crinkled hands, murmuring things like, "What a pretty girl you are, so sweet, so nice." She caresses my hair, runs her hand up and down my back, soothes away my misery with her touch.

I haven't felt like this in a long time, this little girl feeling of being nurtured, cherished, even loved. I have an urge to cry, but all my tears dried up the first night I spent in this ward. Instead, there is a contented grin spreading across my heart.

"Rest now, sweetie," the old woman says. "Everything is going to be all right. Don't you worry about a thing."

And for the moment, I don't.

"DON'T TOUCH ME!!! GET YOUR GODDAMN HANDS OFF OF ME!!! LET ME GO, YOU SONS OF BITCH-ES!!!"

Evelyn is shouting at the top of her lungs, swinging violent arms at two large male attendants who are trying to keep her still. "Ma'am, you need to calm down," says one of the attendants.

"FUCK YOU, YOU PIECE OF SHIT!!! I TOLD YOU NOT TO TOUCH ME!!! LET ME GO!!!"

The two attendants somehow drag her down the hall and into the room she shares with two other women. I ask one of the other patients to push my wheelchair closer, needing to know what is going on. Another big man hurries past me, carrying thick straps in his hands. Five or so able-bodied steps before the doorway, I sit in my wheelchair and watch all three men restraining Evelyn onto her bed with the straps, buckling her up nice and tight in order to prevent escape. Or maybe they just don't want her to hurt anybody, including herself.

A female nurse enters carrying a hypodermic needle. She bends over a raging Evelyn, saying, "This will make you feel a whole lot better."

Evelyn instantly calms down, moaning just a little.

Before leaving the room, the nurse asks, "Is there anything else you guys need?"

The men shake their heads no, and one of them says, "We've got everything else under control. Thanks for your help."

The nurse turns back around, notices me with the patient who was kind enough to wheel me close, and says, "There's nothing for you to see here. You both need to return to the dining hall."

"Is Evelyn OK?" I ask the nurse.

"She's going to be just fine."

I need to know more. "What happened?"

"That's none of your concern. Now come on, I'll escort you back."

The nurse moves behind me, grabs a hold of the handles in the back of my wheelchair and maneuvers me around in

126

the opposite direction. I twist my neck to the far right, so that I can get one last glimpse of Evelyn. She looks tranquil lying there, strapped in her bed, her glazed eyes staring at nothing.

I wonder what pushed her over the edge?

Shrugging to myself, I face forward, watching the dimly lit hallway stretch out before me. My stomach begins to grumble, and I am now looking forward to my previously forgotten dinner, though thoughts of Evelyn linger in my mind.

On a day like any other, my mom has come to visit me. I have recently been infused with more Dilaudid, and am really happy to see her.

"Jasim really misses you," my mother announces from her seat next to me on one of the couches near the back of the TV room.

"That's nice," I say. "Tell him I miss him, too." I'm not sure if I sound convincing, for I have barely thought about him beyond a distant memory of a beautiful, vibrant little boy who is much better off without me.

"Too bad he is not allowed to visit you here. But I talked to one of the hospital workers, and she said you might be able to request outdoor privileges and leave the hospital for a little while. Maybe then you can visit Jasim outside." She looks to see if I'm interested.

"I think it's better if he doesn't see me right now," I say without emotion. "I'm sure he'd freak out if he saw me like this," and I motion to my crippled self, with hands and feet that are capable of nothing.

A flash of sorrow passes through

my mother's eyes, but all she has to say is, "Well, all right. Just let me know if you change your mind."

We fumble for words, until my mom comes up with, "You know that police officer, Nick, the one who sat and talked with you in your apartment?" She is referring to one of the campus cops who broke into my apartment recently, when my family was terrified that I might try to kill myself after this new lupus flare-up had taken away all the feeling in my hands and feet. Nick sat with me for a long while, helped me smoke a cigarette, and talked me into checking myself into a psychiatric ward. In the end, this is where I ended up, in the hotel for the elderly insane.

My mom continues, "Well, Nick asked for your permission to come and visit you here. Would that be okay with you?"

"No, I don't want him to see me like this," I say with finality. While I stare at my pale, skinny legs, my mom says nothing. After another long pause, I tell her, "I could really use a cigarette right now. It's been over a week since I've had one."

"They won't let you go out on the patio and smoke?" she asks, pointing to the back of the room.

"No. They say it's against the rules to allow any of their patients to smoke."

"Let's try, anyway. We can smoke out on the patio, and if we get caught, then we'll just put out our cigarettes and apologize."

One thing I have always loved about my mom is her innate rebel spirit. I usually follow suit, but this time I decline her offer. "No, I don't want to get in trouble. They might decide not to let me have any outdoor privileges, after all."

Mom offers up another scenario in

an effort to beat the rules. "Why don't we ask if you can have those outdoor privileges now, and you can smoke when we go outside?"

I think about her plan for a few seconds, and ultimately respond with, "Okay. It's worth a shot."

She calls over a nurse who has been lurking nearby. "Excuse me," she tells the nurse. "I want to find out if my daughter has outdoor privileges yet."

"Are you taking her out to smoke?"

"No, why do you ask?" my mom says with an innocent lift of her brows.

"Because, your daughter and her friend Evelyn keep insisting that they be allowed to smoke. Because of that, the doctors have instructed us not to let either of them have any outdoor privileges."

"That's ridiculous! She's an adult, and should be allowed to smoke if she wants to!"

"I'm sorry, ma'am. Doctors orders."

"Well, I'm not taking her out to smoke. She just wants to get some fresh air."

"She can get fresh air out on the patio."

Frustrated, my mom turns her back on the nurse, effectively dismissing her.

I chuckle lightly and remark, "Nice try, Mom."

"We want to smoke! We want to smoke! We want to smoke!"

Evelyn and I are raising hell throughout the corridors and communal rooms of our geriatric prison. I am seated in my wheelchair, and Evelyn is pushing me with trembling hands. What a pair we make! A crippled lupus girl and a spastic Parkinson's old lady. I wish someone would record us like this.

The words change slightly, through Evelyn's direction. "We want cigarettes! We want cigarettes! We want cigarettes!"

A nurse administering medicine to patients out of her rolling cart rolls her eyes at us. "You know you're not allowed to smoke while you are a patient here," she says unnecessarily. "Smoking is bad for your health, and this is a hospital. It would be hypocritical for us to allow you to smoke, when it's our job to help you get better."

I lift by left eyebrow and say, "Oh, so we're not allowed to smoke, but it's okay to dope us up with all of those drugs." I motion to the cart in front of her.

"Yeah!" adds Evelyn. "Please explain how being loaded with drugs all day is good for our health, but smoking one lousy cigarette isn't!"

The nurse smiles broadly and shakes her head, but wisely decides not to respond to our brilliant logic.

"Speaking of drugs, have you prepared my afternoon concoction yet?" asks Evelyn.

"Not yet," says the drug-pushing nurse. "I have to take care of a few other patients first."

"What about me?" I ask. "I'm about ready for another Dilaudid fix."

"You'll be after Evelyn," she tells me in no uncertain terms.

Evelyn leans her head down towards me and says, "What do you say we make one more round while we wait?"

"Sounds good!"

She wheels me in the opposite direction, towards the wide corridor lining the rooms we sleep in, and off we go, two kindred junkies with a purpose.

"We want to smoke! We want to

smoke! We want to smoke!"

The days continue bleeding into one. My only time markers are the hours leading up to the next round of medication, the next meal, the next bout of exhaustion that finally forces me to go to sleep at night, the next sunrise creeping around the edge of my curtains.

I awake in a rush, thinking about death. I am lying on my stomach on top of sheets that are starting to wilt from my sweat and despair, staring at the night-stand, with its solitary drawer containing a bottle of Vicodin I brought with me from home. I wonder if twenty pills would be enough to make my heart explode in a massive coronary combustion. Unfortunately, lacking hands capable of opening a child-proof bottle, or anybody compassionate enough to imitate Dr. Kevorkian, the closest I can come to death these days is in my fantasies. Not even my illness will give me a break. The 60 mg of prednisone they are forcing me to take is keeping my flare-up barely in check. *Just my luck.*

Before the next swirl of panic can leave me more broken than I already am, a nurse enters my room to administer another humane dose of Dilaudid into my nervous system. My thoughts are immediately tempered by the needle's first contact with skin. A half hour later I am as near to a state of blissfulness as I can get.

It is a Sunday, and I am uncomfortably situated in a tan padded chair with a prime view of the television set. I am surrounded by many other patients. My stepfather, Herman, is also here, so out of place in these surroundings, with his casual but expensive blue jeans, white long-sleeved button-down shirt, plaid wool jacket and black hipster cap. He has come to watch the NFL semi-finals with me. It's the Tennessee Titans versus our own Oakland Raiders.

"Go Raiders!" I shout into the excitement shimmering like starbursts all around me. "We're going to make it to the Super Bowl this year! I just know it!"

An old black man wearing a t-shirt reading "Real Men Wear Black" nods in agreement. "This will be the year," he says with his deep, gravelly tones. "It's been eighteen years since our last win. I've waited a long time to see it happen again."

"Well, you'll only have to wait one more week," Evelyn throws in, "because today we're gonna kick Tennessee's ass!"

Falling into Place

A sound of cheers rises in the air. Herman is the only one calmly sitting down, not caught up in the ripples of frenzy that all of the elderly patients, plus myself and the hospital staff, are feeling. He is speaking words to match our shouts in meaning, but not in modulation. Phrases like, "Go Raiders," and "Come on, you can do it," don't ring with quite the same enthusiasm when spoken by Herman. They sound bland, instead.

"I know you," an ancient-looking black woman with a shiny brown wig announces. She's nudging Herman's arm, commanding his undivided attention.

"Yeah, I'm Xochi's stepfather," he tells her. "My name is Herman."

"You're from St. Louis, aren't you?" she asks.

"No, I'm from Tallahassee, Florida."

The woman squints her eyes slightly, trying to get a better look at Herman. 'No, you're from St. Louis. You used to be my preacher when I was just a girl."

"I think you've got me confused with somebody else," Herman says without cracking a smile. Without laughing hysterically as I am oh-so-tempted to do.

"No, no," the old lady assures him. "I'm positive that you were my preacher when I was younger. I used to go to your church every Sunday."

You never know. In Herman's prior lifetime, perhaps he really was her preacher. Rather than voice my thoughts out loud, I turn to my stepfather with a huge grin. I say, "Herman, welcome to *Rock Bottom.*"

He looks at me, and in that instant of awareness glinting in his eyes, it is as if Herman knows exactly what I am talking about. It is as if he truly understands.

Falling into Place

The Raiders end up winning, and the next day, a doctor from my ward tells me, "It is time for you to transfer to the physical therapy floor. There's nothing more we can do for you here. You need to be around specialists who can help you return some of the basic motor functions you have lost."

A group of us are seated around a rectangular table inside a small conference room I have never noticed before, towards the back of the dining room. Along with the geriatrics doctor and myself, there is a geriatrics nurse I see more often than the other nurses, a doctor from the physical therapy ward, two physical therapists, and a psychiatrist who occasionally checks in on me.

"Can't I get physical therapy from

here?" I ask. "I thought that was what we had originally discussed. I remember a couple of different physical therapists coming to work with me my first few days here, but then they stopped coming."

"That's because you were very un-cooperative, and so they gave up," says the geriatrics doctor.

The doctor from physical therapy clears her throat and adds, "It was also difficult for the therapists to work with you in this ward, without an exercise room and all of the necessary equipment they generally use to work with our pa-tients, such as exercise balls, bicycles and weights."

"Can't you bring some of that stuff here?" I ask. "Surely the weights could be carried down – I mean, it's not like I need weights that are that heavy. Or what about an exercise ball? If I promise to be cooperative, can't we try this again?"

The geriatrics doctor shakes his head, but it is the psychiatrist who says, "We just can't continue to justify your remaining in this facility. Your physical health is not showing any signs of improvement, and that is the most pressing matter, for now. At this point, what you really need is physical therapy."

"Can't I at least stay here one more week? One week is all I ask. Please."

The other members of our private meeting look at each other in shared agreement, all wearing frowns on their somber faces. The nurse is the only one to reveal a look of sympathy in her dark brown eyes, a slight regret over what must be done. I now understand that my pleas are futile.

It is the geriatrics doctor who delivers the bad news. "I'm sorry, but you'll be transferred to physical therapy tomorrow."

My lungs start to seize in contracting heaves, and my world of pretend comes crashing down.

I feel inconsolable, a boat without motor or sail, adrift in the very center of a vast expanse of foamless ocean, with nothing but sea monsters to keep me company. The geriatrics doctor seems to take pity on me as he allows for a higher dose of Dilaudid to be administered, to help ease the pain. I doubt if anyone here knows that the physical aches became irrelevant long before I entered the facility, when I first learned to let go of my body, to rise above it and take aerial flight. But they must know that I have at least been exaggerating my ailments, if not filling their ears with outright lies.

Right now, there is no amount of

medication, short of a dose strong enough to kill me, that can pull me out of the low levels to which I have sunk. I am *really* not yet ready to leave this place. It is not a simple matter of my unwillingness to face the harsh reality of my physical condition. It's more like being tossed into the deep end before I am allowed to catch a fortifying breath, when I still don't even know how to swim.

"Why don't you come and play Bingo with us," Evelyn calls out from the dining table. "It will help you take your mind off of things. And we can make the most of our last night together."

Without asking, a nurse pushes my wheelchair from its stance near the television set to the large floor space nearby that is reserved for eating our meals. I am brought to a stop in front of an empty place at the table beside Evelyn. The nurse has a gentle smile plastered on her face, and asks, "Would you like an extra chocolate pudding?"

"Sure," I say, before watching her head off to the kitchen.

Evelyn places an empty Bingo card before me. Since I cannot maneuver the small plastic chips onto the numbered squares, she plays my card for me, along with her own, her hands slightly shaking.

"I-25!" calls out a female attendant. "I-25!"

Evelyn looks over both of our cards. "Ooh! I have I-25 on my card!" She covers the number with a plastic chip.

"O-74!" Half a dozen heartbeats go by. "O-74!"

The nurse comes back with my chocolate pudding. "Here you go, honey," she says. I now have a plastic band secured with Velcro around the center of my right hand, with slots on either side for holding eating utensils. A spoon is inserted, and I begin the tedious task of feeding myself like a baby – messy face and all.

"G-48, G-48!"

"That's one of my numbers!" says Evelyn. "And, oh look! You have it, too!" She places plastic chips on each of our cards, glances at me, then dips a paper napkin into a glass of water before quickly wiping chocolate off of my face.

"B-9!"

Evelyn skims the cards. "BIN-GO!!!" She jumps up and down and throws her arms heavenward. "I won! I won! Look how lucky I am! So, what's my prize?"

The attendant in charge of calling out the numbers hands Evelyn a small white teddy bear with brown eyes and a red nose; it cradles a book and has ears, feet, wings and a halo all colored in shiny gold. Evelyn then offers her prize

146

to me. "Here you go, beautiful! This is my goodbye present to you, something to remember me by. Of course, we'll visit each other while you're up in physical therapy. And you're coming back for the Super Bowl, aren't you?"

"Of course," I say, forcing a wobbly smile to my lips.

"Aww, honey, don't look so sad. You should be happy to get out of here, away from all these nut cases! And just think, you'll finally get to see your son again, since he's allowed up in physical therapy."

I say nothing, clutching the bear to my chest with my forearms.

"What are you going to name her?" Evelyn asks.

"I don't know yet."

"What about 'Lucky Bingo', in honor of how I won her for you?"

"I like that. I like it a lot," I say, thinking for a moment. "But I want to include your name, so maybe I'll call her 'Evelyn Lucky Bingo Angel Bear'."

"HA HA HA!!! I love it! Evelyn Lucky Bingo Angel Bear! That's a great name to remember me by, so you'll never forget our very last night together in this loony bin! But like I said, we'll keep in touch when you're gone."

"Of course we will!" And I almost convince myself this is so, that this chapter of my life is not yet over, even as I feel a hint of tears forming in my eyes.

Epilogue

Change, it is often said, is the only constant. My journey with lupus has continued, marked by ebbs and flows, remissions and flares, acute and chronic phases. Things improved, worsened, remained steady. I went in and out of hospital and institutional care. Despite the constant interruptions, I completed my B.A. cum laude at the University of California, Berkeley, majoring in Peace and Conflict Studies, and an MFA in Creative Writing at St. Mary's College.

My son Jasim showed musical promise at a young age. I devoted myself to finding the right teachers, driving him to classes, listening to him practice, shepherding his performance schedule, and taking pleasure in his budding talent. I would love to have done more for him, but my lupus prevented me. Still, I am proud that Jasim has blossomed as a musician and is currently completing a music degree at The Julliard School in New York.

Unfortunately, my life did not develop as I had hoped. After my last big lupus flare in 2012 I developed inflammation in my brain as well as antiphospholipid antibodies—a syndrome associated with lupus that in my case led to multiple strokes. I am now permanently paralyzed, unable to walk or unbend my right arm, and reside in an assisted living facility. Life sucks for me but I'm so proud of my son who was recently accepted into the Master's program at The Juilliard School. Jasim has been my greatest accomplishment in life. And for now that is good enough.

Acknowledgements

I owe my appreciation and thanks to those who made the publication of this book possible. Thank you to Anne Gray Brown, Lata Mani and Rosa-Linda Fregoso for their terrific guidance, generous suggestions, and detailed reading of the manuscript.

About the Author

Xochitl M. Perales was born in Corpus Christi, Texas on "cinco de mayo" (May 5th), 1973. Her name, Xochitl, means "flower" in Nahuatl, the language of the Mexicas, the indigenous people of the Valley of Mexico who were the rulers of the Aztec empire.

At an early age, Xochitl moved with her mother to Austin, Texas and three years later to San Diego and then Santa Barbara, California. She has lived in New Hampshire, Madrid, Salamanca, Granada, and in the early 1990s settled in the Bay Area of California.

In 1998, Xochitl was diagnosed with lupus during her third trimester of pregnancy. Despite this debilitating autoimmune illness, she raised her son, Jasim, as a single parent. She even completed a bachelor's degree with honors from the University of California, Berkeley in 2005, majoring in Peace and Conflict Studies; and in 2010 a Master of Fine Arts in Creative Writing from Saint Mary's College. Xochitl has also traveled extensively with her young son, visiting India, Nepal, France, Italy, Spain, Portugal, Jamaica, Costa Rica, and Mexico.

After a lupus flare in 2012, she developed antiphospholipid-antibodies syndrome (APS), a disorder that causes blood clots. Xochitl had a series of strokes and is currently paralyzed. She resides in an assisted living facility in Oakland California. Her pride and joy is her son, Jasim Perales, an accomplished jazz trombone player who graduated from The Juilliard School.

Xochitl started writing poetry in elementary school. *Falling into Place* is based on her master's thesis. She is working on a full length memoir.